Fishermen's Wool is  l.
This worsted weight (Jil,
which protects the wool from the elements. Perfect
for winter garments and accessories, Fishermen's
Wool can also be dyed or felted. Soft, supple and
utterly elegant, Fishermen's Wool is perfect for
everything from fashion pieces to cozy home accents.
Great stitch definition makes it perfect for cables and
other textural patterns and the 100% wool content
makes it fabulous for felting.

About Lion Brand® Yarn Company

Lion Brand Yarn Company is America's oldest hand knitting yarn brand. Founded in 1878, Lion Brand Yarn Company is a leading supplier of quality hand knitting and crochet yarns. Throughout its history, Lion Brand Yarn has been at the forefront of yarn trends while consistently providing its customers with the highest quality product at a value price. The company's mission is to provide ideas, inspiration and education to yarn crafters.

LACE SCARF

■■■■□ INTERMEDIATE

SIZE
About 9 x 69 in. (23 x 175.5 cm)

MATERIALS
LION BRAND® FISHERMEN'S WOOL
> #126 Nature's Brown 1 skein (A)
> #123 Oatmeal 1 skein (B)
> #098 Natural 1 skein (C)
> or colors of your choice

LION BRAND knitting needles size 9 (5.5 mm)
LION BRAND large-eyed blunt needle

GAUGE
18 sts + 20 rows = 4 in. (10 cm) in Pattern st.
BE SURE TO CHECK YOUR GAUGE.

> **TIP**
> Knitting Necessities: To avoid dropped stitches, always try to complete the row you are working on before you put down your knitting.

PATTERN STITCH (multiple of 12 sts + 6)
Row 1: K3, *yo, k2tog; rep from * to last 3 sts, k3.

Rows 2 and 4: K3, p to last 3 sts, k3.

Row 3: Knit.

Rows 5 and 8: K3, *k3tog, k4, yo, k1, yo, k4; rep from * to last 3 sts, k3.

Rows 6, 7 and 9: K3, *p3tog, p4, yo, p1, yo, p4; rep from * to last 3 sts, k3.

Rows 10–18: Rep Rows 1-9.
Rep Rows 1–18 for Pattern stitch.

COLOR SEQUENCE
Work *18 rows with A, 18 rows with B, 18 rows with C; rep from *.

SCARF
With A, cast on 42 sts.
Beg with Row 1, work in Pattern stitch and Color Sequence until Scarf measures about 65 in. (165 cm) from beg, or 3½ in. (9 cm) less than desired length, end with 18 rows with C. Change to A, work Rows 1–18 of Pattern stitch. Bind off.

FINISHING
Weave in ends.

WINDY CITY TOTE

Shown on page 7.

 EASY

SIZE
About 9½ x 14 in. (24 x 35.5 cm) after felting

MATERIALS
LION BRAND® FISHERMEN'S WOOL
    #126 Nature's Brown 1 ball (A)
    #123 Oatmeal 1 ball (B)
    or colors of your choice
LION BRAND knitting needles size 10½ (6.5 mm)

GAUGE
16 sts + 20 rows = 4 in. (10 cm) in St st (k on RS, p on WS)
before felting.
BE SURE TO CHECK YOUR GAUGE.

> **TIP**
> When combining two yarns, decide how you
> want your finished piece to look. For a subtle
> effect, choose two colors that are close in tone
> to each other. A more graphic look can be
> achieved by picking contrasting colors.

TOTE
With A, cast on 86 sts.

Rows 1-5: With A, work in St st (k on RS, p on WS).

Rows 6-10: With B, work in St st.
Rep Rows 1-10, 21 more times, then rep Rows 1-5 once.
Bind off.

HANDLES (make 2)
With A, cast on 7 sts. Work in St st until piece measures
35 in. (89 cm) from beginning. Bind off.

FINISHING
Fold Tote in half and sew side seams. Fold up corners and
sew in place. Sew Handles to Tote 5 in. (12.5 cm) from sides
and 3 in. (7.5 cm) below top edge. Weave in ends.

FELTING
Wash by machine on a hot wash/cold rinse cycle with
detergent and several pieces of clothing to agitate. To felt
additionally, dry by machine on a regular setting until
almost dry. Remove from dryer and pull into shape.

WARM UP HAT

◼◼◻◻◻ EASY +

SIZE
S (M, L, 1X)

Finished Circumference
19½ (20¼, 22¼, 23¼) in. (49.5 (51.5, 56.5, 59) cm)

Note: Pattern is written for smallest size with changes for larger sizes in parentheses. When only one number is given, it applies to all sizes. To follow pattern more easily, circle all numbers pertaining to your size before beginning.

MATERIALS
LION BRAND® FISHERMEN'S WOOL
    #123 Oatmeal 1 skein (A)
    #126 Nature's Brown 1 skein (B)
    or colors of your choice
LION BRAND knitting needles size 9 (5.5 mm)
LION BRAND large-eyed blunt needle
LION BRAND stitch holder

TIP

Before you begin a project

1. Make a copy of your pattern and put the original in a safe place.

2. Read through your pattern, circling the number of stitches for your size.

3. On a 3" x 5" card write out any unfamiliar abbreviations and use the card to mark your place in the pattern.

GAUGE

16 sts + 24 rows = 4 in. (10 cm) in St st (k on RS, p on WS)
BE SURE TO CHECK YOUR GAUGE.

STITCH EXPLANATION
K1, p1 Rib

Row 1: *K1, p1; rep from * across.

Row 2: K the knit sts and p the purl sts.
Rep Row 2 for K1, p1 Rib.

HAT
Earflaps

With A, cast on 3 sts. Work in k1, p1 Rib until piece measures 8 in. (20.5 cm) from beginning, ending with a WS row.

Row 1 (RS): K1, (k1, yo, k1) into next st, k1 – 5 sts.

Row 2 and all WS rows: Purl.

Row 3: K2, (k1, yo, k1) into next st, k to end – 7 sts.

Row 5: K3, (k1, yo, k1) into next st, k to end – 9 sts.

Row 7: K4, (k1, yo, k1) into next st, k to end – 11 sts.
Continue as established, increasing 2 sts in center st of each RS row until you have a total of 23 sts, ending with a WS row. Sl sts onto a holder.

Rep for second Earflap, but do not sl sts to a holder.

Join for Hat

Continuing on same needle as second Earflap, with A, cast on 6 (8, 10, 11) sts.

Next Row (Joining Row): K across cast-on sts, k23 Earflap sts, cast on 19 (19, 23, 25) sts, k23 Earflap sts from holder, cast on 6 (8, 10, 11) sts – 77 (81, 89, 93) sts.

Work even in St st until piece measures 5 (5½, 6, 6½) in. (12.5 (14, 15, 16.5) cm), from Joining Row, end with a RS row.

Next Row: Purl, decrease (1, 1, 5) times evenly spaced across row – 72 (80, 88, 88) sts.

Shape Crown
Row 1 (RS): *K6, k2tog; rep from * across– 63 (70, 77, 77) sts.

Row 2 and WS rows: Purl.

Row 3: *K5, k2tog; rep from * across – 54 (60, 66, 66) sts.

Row 5: *K4, k2tog; rep from * across – 45 (50, 55, 55) sts.

Row 7: *K3, k2tog; rep from * across – 36 (40, 44, 44) sts.

Row 9: *K2, k2tog; rep from * across – 27 (30, 33, 33) sts.

Row 11: *K1, k2tog; rep from * across – 18 (20, 22, 22) sts.

Row 13: K2tog across – 9 (10, 11, 11) sts.

Row 15: K2tog across, end k1 (0, 1, 1) – 5 (5, 6, 6) sts.
Cut yarn, leaving a 12 in. (30.5 cm) tail. Thread tail through remaining sts and pull to gather. Knot tightly to secure.

FINISHING
Sew seam. With a doubled strand of B and large-eyed needle, work Blanket Stitch around entire edge of Hat and Earflaps. Weave in ends.

ZIG ZAG TWEED SCARF

◖◼◻◻◻ EASY

SIZE
About 6 x 60 in. (15 x 152.5 cm)

MATERIALS
LION BRAND® FISHERMEN'S WOOL
>   #200 Oak Tweed 1 skein
>   or color of your choice

LION BRAND knitting needles size 10 1/2 (6.5 mm)
LION BRAND large-eyed blunt needle

GAUGE
14 stitches = 4 in. (10 cm) in Garter st (k every row)
with 2 strands held tog.
BE SURE TO CHECK YOUR GAUGE.

> **TIP**
>
> When your tension varies as you knit or crochet it may be that you are concentrating too much on the work and not letting it flow naturally in a rhythmic movement. Try listening to a book on tape as you knit. You'll be able to follow what you are doing, but your tension may even out, as your focus is more even and relaxed.

STITCH EXPLANATION
Kfb (inc 1 st) Knit next st without removing it from left needle, then k through back of same st.

NOTES
1. Scarf is worked with 2 strands of yarn held tog throughout.
2. Wind yarn into 2 balls before beginning.

SCARF
With 2 strands of yarn held together, cast on 2 sts.

Inc Row: K to last st, kfb in last st – 3 sts.
Rep Inc Row until you have a total of 19 sts.

Dec Row: K to last 2 sts, k2tog – 18 sts.
Rep Dec Row until 9 sts rem.
Continue to inc to 19 sts and dec to 9 sts until piece measures about 60 in. (152.5 cm) from beginning, end with 9 sts. Rep Dec Row until 2 sts rem.
K2tog. Cut yarn and pull through rem loop.

FINISHING
Weave in ends.

STARBOARD HAT

Shown on page 17.

 BEGINNER

SIZE
One size, will stretch to fit a range of sizes.

Finished Circumference
About 19 in. (48.5 cm).

MATERIALS
LION BRAND® FISHERMEN'S WOOL
   #123 Oatmeal 1 skein
   or color of your choice
LION BRAND crochet hook size P-15 (10 mm)
LION BRAND large-eyed blunt needle
LION BRAND pompom maker

GAUGE
8 stitches = 4 in. (10 cm) in pattern.
BE SURE TO CHECK YOUR GAUGE.

> **TIP**
> If you are crocheting too tightly, perhaps you are not sliding the work back far enough onto the hook.

NOTES
1. Hat is worked with 2 strands of yarn held together throughout.
2. Wind yarn into 2 balls before beginning.

HAT
With 2 strands of yarn held together, chain 39.

Row 1: Single crochet in 2nd chain from hook, double crochet in next chain, *single crochet in next chain, double crochet in next chain; repeat from * across, end with a double crochet in last chain – 38 stitches.

Row 2: Chain 1, turn, *single crochet in next double crochet, double crochet in next single crochet; repeat from * across.
Repeat Row 2 until piece measures 9 in. (23 cm) from beginning. Fasten off.

FINISHING
Seam sides together. Thread yarn through each stitch of last row and pull to gather. Knot securely.
Following package directions, make a pompom and tie to top of Hat.
Weave in ends.

ASHFORD SHAWL

■◘☐☐◗ BEGINNER

SIZE
About 20 x 60 in. (51 x 152.5 cm)

MATERIALS
LION BRAND® FISHERMEN'S WOOL
#123 Oatmeal 2 skeins
or color of your choice
LION BRAND knitting needles size 8 (5 mm)
LION BRAND large-eyed blunt needle

GAUGE
18 stitches + 22 rows = 4 in. (10 cm) in Pattern stitch.
EXACT GAUGE IS NOT ESSENTIAL FOR THIS PROJECT.

SHAWL
Cast on 91 stitches.

Row 1: Knit 1, *purl 1, knit 1; repeat from * across.

Row 2: Knit.
Repeat Rows 1 and 2 until almost all yarn has been used.
Bind off.

FINISHING
Weave in ends.

> **TIP**
> If you wind your yarn into a ball before using it, you can store it in a plastic zip-lock bag with the yarn label on the inside of the bag. When you are ready to use it, the yarn will be clean and untangled. Pull the yarn from the top of the bag or cut (or punch) a hole in the bag and flow it through the hole.

CLOUD CASCADE SCARF

◖☐☐☐▷ BEGINNER

SIZE
About 4 x 70 in. (10 x 178 cm)

MATERIALS
LION BRAND® FISHERMEN'S WOOL
#200 Oak Tweed 1 skein
or color of your choice
LION BRAND crochet hook size N-13 (9 mm)
LION BRAND large-eyed blunt needle

GAUGE
12 double crochet = 4 in. (10 cm) with 2 strands held together.
BE SURE TO CHECK YOUR GAUGE.

> TIP
> Helpful Hint: For an extra special gift, involve the gift recipient in choosing the colors.

NOTES

1. Scarf is worked with 2 strands of yarn held together throughout.
2. Wind yarn into 2 balls before beginning.

SCARF

With 2 strands of yarn held together, chain 110.

Row 1: Double crochet in 4th chain from hook, *double crochet in next chain, 2 double crochet in next chain; repeat from * across.

Row 2: Chain 3, turn, double crochet in same space, *double crochet in next 2 double crochet, 2 double crochet in next double crochet; repeat from * across.

Row 3: Chain 3, turn, double crochet in same space, *double crochet in next 3 double crochet, 2 double crochet in next double crochet; repeat from * across.

Row 4: Chain 3, turn, double crochet in same space, *double crochet in next 4 double crochet, 2 double crochet in next double crochet; repeat from * across
Fasten off.

FINISHING

Weave in ends.

GENERAL INSTRUCTIONS

ABBREVIATIONS

beg = begin(ning)
cm = centimeters
dec = decreas(e)(s)(ing)
dc = double crochet
k = knit
kfb = knit front and back
k2tog = knit 2 together
p = purl
mm = millimeters
rem = remain(s)(ing)
rep = repeat(s)(ing
RS = right side
sl = slip
st(s) = stitch(es)
St st = Stockinette stitch
tog = together
tr = treble (triple) crochet
WS = wrong side
yo = yarn over

* — When you see an asterisk used within a pattern row, the symbol indicates that later you will be told to repeat a portion of the instruction. Most often the instructions will say, repeat from * so many times.

( ) or [ ] — Set off a short number of stitches that are repeated or indicated additional information.

GAUGE

Never underestimate the importance of gauge. Achieving the correct gauge assures that the finished size of your piece matches the finished size given in the pattern.

CHECKING YOUR GAUGE

Work a swatch that is at least 4" (10 cm) square. Use the suggested needle or hook size and the number of stitches given. If your swatch is larger than 4" (10 cm), you need to work it again using a smaller hook; if it is smaller than 4" (10 cm), try it with a larger hook. The same concept applies if you are knitting. If your swatch is larger, work it again with smaller needles. If your swatch is larger, try smaller needles. This might require a swatch or two to get the exact gauge given in the pattern.

METRICS

As a handy reference, keep in mind that 1 ounce = approximately 28 grams and 1" = 2.5 centimeters.

TERMS

continue in this way or as established — Once a pattern is set up (established), the instructions may tell you to continue in the same way.

fasten off — To end your piece, you need to simply pull the yarn through the last loop left on the hook. This keeps the last stitch intact and prevents the work from unraveling.

right side — Refers to the front of the piece.

work even — This is used to indicate an area worked as established without increasing or decreasing.

KNIT TERMINOLOGY

UNITED STATES		INTERNATIONAL
gauge	=	tension
bind off	=	cast off
yarn over (YO)	=	yarn forward (yfwd) **or** yarn around needle (yrn)

CROCHET TERMINOLOGY

UNITED STATES		INTERNATIONAL
slip stitch (slip st)	=	single crochet (sc)
single crochet (sc)	=	double crochet (dc)
half double crochet (hdc)	=	half treble crochet (htr)
double crochet (dc)	=	treble crochet (tr)
treble crochet (tr)	=	double treble crochet (dtr)
double treble crochet (dtr)	=	triple treble crochet (ttr)
triple treble crochet (tr tr)	=	quadruple treble crochet (qtr)
skip	=	miss

Yarn Weight Symbol & Names	SUPER FINE 1	FINE 2	LIGHT 3	MEDIUM 4	BULKY 5	SUPER BULKY 6
Type of Yarns in Category	Sock, Fingering Baby	Sport, Baby	DK, Light Worsted	Worsted, Afghan, Aran	Chunky, Craft, Rug	Bulky, Roving
Knit Gauge Ranges in Stockinette St to 4" (10 cm)	27-32 sts	23-26 sts	21-24 sts	16-20 sts	12-15 sts	6-11 sts
Advised Needle Size Range	1-3	3-5	5-7	7-9	9-11	11 and larger
Crochet Gauge Ranges in Single Crochet to 4" (10 cm)	21-32 sts	16-20 sts	12-17 sts	11-14 sts	8-11 sts	5-9 sts
Advised Hook Size Range	B-1 to E-4	E-4 to 7	7 to I-9	I-9 to K-10.5	K-10.5 to M-13	M-13 and larger

KNIT IN THE FRONT AND INTO THE BACK
(abbreviated kfb)

Knit the next stitch but do not slip the old stitch off the left needle(Fig. 1a). Insert the right needle into the back loop of the same stitch and knit it (Fig. 1b), then slip the old stitch off the left needle.

Fig. 1a

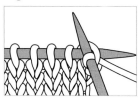

Fig. 1b

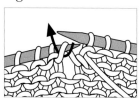

KNIT 2 TOGETHER (abbreviated k2tog)

Insert the right needle into the front of the first two stitches on the left needle as if to knit (Fig. 2), then knit them together as if they were one stitch.

Fig. 2

KNIT 3 TOGETHER (abbreviated k3tog)

Insert the right needle into the front of the first three stitches on the left needle as if to knit (Fig. 3), then knit them together as if they were one stitch.

Fig. 3

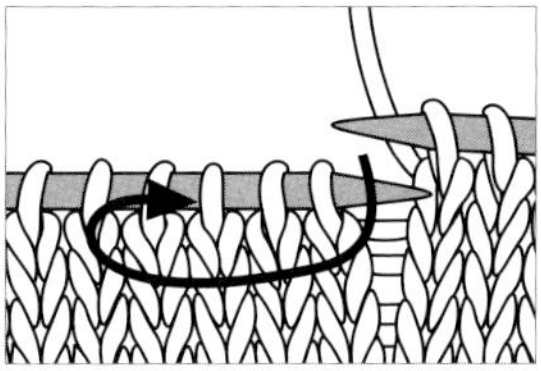

YARN OVER (abbreviated yo)
After a knit stitch, before a knit stitch

Bring the yarn forward between the needles, then back over the top of the right hand needle, so that it is now in position to knit the next stitch (Fig. 4a).

After a purl stitch, before a purl stitch

Take yarn over the right hand needle to the back, then forward under it, so that it is now in position to purl the next stitch (Fig. 4b).

Fig. 4a

Fig. 4b

KNITTING NEEDLES

UNITED STATES	ENGLISH U.K.	METRIC (mm)
0	13	2
1	12	2.25
2	11	2.75
3	10	3.25
4	9	3.5
5	8	3.75
6	7	4
7	6	4.5
8	5	5
9	4	5.5
10	3	6
10½	2	6.5
11	1	8
13	00	9
15	000	10
17	---	12.75

CROCHET HOOKS

UNITED STATES	METRIC (mm)
B-1	2.25
C-2	2.75
D-3	3.25
E-4	3.5
F-5	3.75
G-6	4
H-8	5
I-9	5.5
J-10	6
K-10½	6.5
N	9
P	10
Q	15

We have made every effort to ensure that these instructions are accurate and complete. We cannot, however, be responsible for human error, typographical mistakes, or variations in individual work.